GW01385450

ON A KNIFE EDGE

E R R A T A

Front cover photo: We acknowledge Tim Royall as the artist of the
work depicted and thank him for the use of his photo

Page 40: The author of 'Every Step' is Philip Baker, not Dide
Siemmond, as incorrectly ascribed. We apologise to both poets

ON A KNIFE EDGE

Poems

Suffolk Poetry Society

ON A KNIFE EDGE

Poems

Suffolk **P**oetry **S**ociety

Cover design: Derek Adams
derek@derek-adams.co.uk

Published by Suffolk Poetry Society

First Edition 2021

ISBN: 978-0-9511789-7-3

suffolkpoetrysociety.org

Printed by Lavenham Press

Contents

Introduction

This collection of poetry has been inspired by the theme of a major exhibition of the art and craft of lettering design and hand letter carving, calligraphy and letterpress mounted in 2021 by the Lettering Arts Trust, entitled *On A Knife Edge*. The exhibition aims to draw attention to the plight of nature in the UK – so many species of plant, insect, bird, mammal which for generations we have taken for granted, yet now feature on the dreaded "Red List" of species, are close to extinction. The very habitats they rely on are also threatened, if not already disappeared from some places.

On A Knife Edge – its art and poetry – signals a clarion call to action, reminding us to respect and cherish the equal place which the natural world holds; reminding us that, with concerted collective will and effort, the perilous predicament of our natural world can still be turned around.

The precious craft of stone letter cutting is also on a knife edge – high on the red list of endangered crafts identified by the Heritage Crafts Association. The Lettering Arts Trust, as a champion of the lettering arts, has a mission to ensure that the art of hand drawn lettering and hand letter cutting is sustained and can continue to flourish.

The poets are members of Suffolk Poetry Society, their brief – to lament such losses visibly on the horizon. However, poets see beyond the horizon and there are poems here which simply express a love of the natural world, how humankind responds to the natural world, for good or ill, celebrating its beauty perceived, its lessons learned, and its safety cherished. Between these covers you will read and, we hope, enjoy poems expressing many facets of a poet's engagement with Nature.

Suffolk Poetry Society thanks the poets for their gracious permission to use the poems in this anthology.

Suffolk Poetry Society

Acknowledgements

Suffolk Poetry Society would like to acknowledge all those who have contributed to the creation of this book, particularly Derek Adams, Lynne Nesbit, Beth Soule and Colin Whyles. Suffolk Poetry Society also thanks the Lettering Arts Trust for inviting its members to create this book to go alongside their exhibition *On A Knife Edge*.

However, the main thanks must, of course, go to our very gifted poets who have graciously and unconditionally offered their poems in response to such an inspiring invitation. Suffolk Poetry Society is grateful to its members for their generous and equally inspiring response.

All proceeds from the sale of this book will be shared between Suffolk Poetry Society and the Lettering Arts Trust.

This Dear Earth

Winter exposes a shrunken space
– plastic bags caught on branches, beer cans
tossed in hedgerows.

Come the spring, when catkins hang like
yellow rain, and the first buds plump up
we tramp the paths relieved, can still see
where we've come from, where we're
heading,
but it's as if the land has shaken itself,
and settled in place, afresh.

The meadows look rested, lush,
ready for summer grazing.
There's cuckoo-spit frothing on blackthorn,
clusters of comfrey, lady's smock
and buttercups, all opening to Suffolk skies.

Eleanor J Vale

White Clover in the Lawn

appears overnight like a sudden hailstorm
soft as pompoms with gingery fringes
and leaves which fan out and touch like fingers.

Already they're busy with buzzing and humming
gauzy wings going and coming.
Gentle gardeners who skimp on mowing
help to keep this traffic flowing.

Margaret Seymour

Podcasting

cusp of dawn
crown of dusk
those husks of time
the intoxicating musk
that invites and entices
leavings of bark and leaf
and fruit suspended
ripe pendulous

perpetual transfer and promotion
nothing is wasted

repollinated seed
refertilised flesh
regorged and resurging

through yellowtail browntail womwood pug
chafer leafcutter ladybirdbug
through cloud-bordered brindle pine hoverfly
snowberry clearwing bright-line brown-eye
through white-letter hairstretch through fletch and foil
and by lugworm toil through sand and soil

and even the shuck and shell
is podcast into still lives
for propagating artists.

Roger West

The Naming of Flowers

As long as children learn the names of flowers
they will live to share the land.

I learned their country names,
the red and yellow of eggs and bacon
a more succulent mouthful
than bird's foot trefoil.

Daffodils with muddled petals,
sturdy natives on short stems,
coltsfoot, celandine and shepherd's purse;
violets in the dry ditch.

Stinking nanny, a puzzling name
for scentless mayweed; lady's smock
in a damp dell, bird's eye,
columbine and keck.

All white and lacy flowers were keck,
from cow parsley to hemlock.
All came with the warning
not to make a whistle from the stem.

Herb Robert, Jack-by-the-hedge,
Bobby's buttons and Aaron's rod,
Good King Henry, Lords and Ladies
danced through my dreams.

And now, if on the verge I see
a single poppy or dog-daisy,
yarrow, vetch or campion,
I am a girl again running through the orchard.

Diane Jackman

4

cuckoo flowers ring
hollow in damp meadow grass –

ghost of ancient pond

Diane Jackman

Metamorphosis

What sets out
as rich in colour, shape and sound

slowly drains
into a less majestic loss of leaf and twig

fades, as animals
slip out one after another

and roars erased
and song and shrieks stifled

and colours
and contours lying slain to nothingness

where only
barren ground remains as a blank chapter

till the sounds
of claxons clatter between new high-rise

glistening vainly
in the gloam of dead shadows.

Jacques Groen

Secheresse

Early april barely budded trees stretch down the scorched streets. Powdered blood and bonemeal in the fields. The dark red disordered rush of poppies runs dry. Dried blood into dried mud. Late august leaves crumpled and curled like parchment on parched pavements. They waft through the windows we keep open to trick the heat into running through and away. The dust and rust of the colours of the land sucked up into bushes and trees. Celery radish asparagus strawberry then broad bean and pea and already the pears and the plums. Market stall produce gallops past like mercury sprinters like relay runners briefly abreast and then gone. And in the supermarkets seasons gathered together corralled and tethered under thermostatic control. Everything here in these arid spaces.

Roger West

Cricket

Cricket in a jam jar
crouched here in my den of fern
What wonder of design created you and I?
And though you are my captive
You show no fear or doubt
that after our discussion
I shall open up the lid
and in a moment you'll be gone
And all that's left the smell of grass
A childhood's memory
Shared knowledge of a Summer's day
that now will not return
That you would go and we must part
and I shan't even see you leave.

Ian Griffiths

Lepidoptera Helicoptera

Papillons de nuit. Butterfly/moth: here in France the distinction is temporal rather than entomological. These early morning night butterflies rotorvate putter-puttering around my head. In my path I find a drowsy cicada. I bend down to rescue him from tractor wheels and I'm struck for a moment by his rusty underwings. A woman passing by misconstrues my hesitation. "Elles ne piquent pas," she says - they don't sting - and she scoops the creature up and into the grassy verge. She tells me how her brother used to push a stick into a cicada's anus and throw it into the air to watch it come helicoptering down. "Whereas I," she says, "know that if you turn a cicada over in your hand and gently stroke its stomach, it will sing for you." When she's gone I lift the cicada from its roadside refuge and try to turn it over in my hand. It resists my efforts, clinging desperately to my fingers with all the genetic mistrust it can muster. "I'm not her brother," I tell it. "Neither are you mine," it replies.

Roger West

Butterfly

A Butterfly beats iridescent wings against the glass
And I concerned at its distress
cup it in the darkness of my palms
feel flutter of its wings
My heart uneasy at the thrill of capture and control
I savour my largesse
The act of letting go
And so I open up my hands and offer it to air.
It for an instant doesn't stir
As if to say it has no need of me
will choose itself when it will leave
that freedom is its right and not my gift
Then it is gone
And I awakened find that I am free

Ian Griffiths

On the morning path
tattered wings, a butterfly
broken. Summer's gone

Elizabeth Soule

Butterfly

A butterfly
lives for only 7 weeks,
experts say.
Time
is relative,
scientists say,
in feeling, blatant,
physics, more surprising,
measurements can be split
in different ways,
along a metronomic beat
or a changing feeling,
70 years fleeing
a breath of wind lifting
a second falling
of our lives flowing.

Dide Siemmond

On encouraging a trapped bee to leave my house
To be a free bee or not

Fran Reader

Where the Bee Sucks

The scent of orange blossom drifts around me
Collecting on my tongue like perfumed nectar
The hum of bees at work invades my hearing
Collecting on my tongue as smooth as beeswax

The summer sunshine fills the nooks and crannies
Collecting on my tongue as vineyards' ripenings
Reminding me of how it is in Heaven
Between my many lives so short and sweet-lived

The scents, the sounds, the sights all honey-tasting
In drops divine pervade my soul's earth raiment
If that was Heaven on some star since forgotten
Then this is Heaven by my earth's senses now remembered

My soul and I with Heaven are face to face
My tongue is sweetened with the taste of grace

Lynne Nesbit

Honey on a knife edge
Sweetness of life and death

Valerie Denton

11

Hedgehog Calling

Snuffling, scrambling,
each night, twenty past nine
a lone figure meanders along the hedge;
always keeping to the edge.
I waited each evening in October
sitting by the window
as though we had an assignation.
I watched his bumbling inspection
like a minor official
nosing meticulously
            each cranny in the stones,
close to each other through the glass.

One evening, no visitor
and one morning at the crossroads
a magnificent hedgehog
flattened by a motorist,
body splayed out like a sunburst
and me the only mourner
in all the empty October evenings.

Pat Jourdan

Hedgehog

Hunched ball of prickles
no protection against cars
roads snatch slug slayers.

Kaaren Whitney

Extinction threatens

Species' closures
Rebellion, exposures
Still lives wane as
Winters freeze to one long hibernation.

Hedgehogs' box unused
No eating of the bulbs
Or upturned pots at night
No snuffling round the door
Are they coming any more?

Valerie Denton

Glow-Worms

Have you seen the glow-worms twinkle?
Rivals to the stars
blinking greetings from pixies and elf
kinds
down where the horses graze.

Have you seen the glow-worms sparkle?
A morse code of sorts
wavering through the coffee air
awakened from the light that falls.

Have you seen the glow-worms glitter?
Boats in the watery sky
Lighthouses that watch the magic
and trouble that lies unheeded high.

Dide Siemmond

Adders

In spring they slide from under the gorse
and when it's warm they're out in force.
They like this place of gravelly sand
where quarry owners wish to expand.

Margaret Seymour

Shadows feed the corners.
Dormouse has lost her
teapot. Unsafe world.

Kate Foley

What can a shrew be, but a shrew
A dormouse only that
And then to take that from them
Starve them from themselves
And shed no tear
No thought
No heed
Just *me*..

Jacques Groen

Wildcat

There he was, thirty feet away
stepping along a drystane wall
at the wildwood's extremity.
He stopped and raised a paw
but not in greeting.
His black-tipped tail swished low
across the lichened stone
and with a flick of it he vanished.

Silver whiskers, eyes of gold,
a trove of priceless treasure
for just seven beats of a heart.

Now when I pass that way it's half
in hope I'll see him there and half in fear
he's gone forever.

Sheila Lockhart

Scottish Wildcat

Homeless, ghosting through
remembered worlds: at our guilt,
your eyes rage and burn

James Knox Whittet

Scottish Wildcat

How fierce she looks
Under her glass dome!

Margaret Seymour

Mustelid Encounter

Pine trees line the lane, their branches waving
In the gloaming. As Moine Mhòr slips from view,
Night extinguishes the final shadows, blotting out
Every tussock and hummock with musty breath.

Mysteries swirl above outcrop and petroglyph;
Ancient lore, embedded in cup and ring marks,
Retains deep secrets. Suddenly two eyes spin
Through thin air. A cream bib bobs up and down,
Ethereal, dreamlike, piercing a membrane of mist.
Night returns, imprinted with stealth.

Caroline Gill

Double Beauty – Minsmere

Water reflects reeds
bending their straightness.
Waders beak to beak
tilt to meet their shimmering selves.
A pair of Linnets hang
one up, one down on a hawthorn.
Two rainbows arc above
one stretches a perfect bow
over spring green woods
its shadow, more subtle,
fades into cloud
where noisy geese
side by side,
impeccably dressed
come sliding down
feet forward, to cleave
the water held sky.

Susan Mobbs

movement stilled beneath
limebright duckweed stagnating
while we skate the surface

Lynne Nesbit

Oystercatcher

ink back
chalk front
Red pencil beak

strides like a teacher
prodding the grass

Margaret Seymour

Four tanka (4-6-4-7-6)

near the lighthouse
sea birds lift over the
lip of the cliff
toying with the ice-cold tides
coming in, going out

puffins pursued
Into their burrows by
bullying gulls
dream of the open sea and
surviving arctic storms

the red squirrel
retreats into wild land
beside the deer
eyeing an empty mountain
and unexpected trees

on a knife edge
this small world balances,
sun on the blade,
wild flower meadows shining
beyond the open gate

Tim Lenton

Sea Change 1950

She kneels by a rockpool, sees
shrimps backfiring, porcelain
crabs scuttling, blancmange anemones –
a toy theatre behind seaweed curtains
made over new at each tide

She is dreaming how the rockpool
opens inward
how she slides through its doorway
to a place where waves dance
in the untouched ocean

Christina Buckton

Seagrass
you ask me
what it's worth

Seagrass is a species suffering severe declines in Suffolk, over
98% of the meadows being lost since the 1960s and 1970s.

Tim Gardiner

Knoydart Dreaming

High tide –
    Sea-pinks bloom
    underwater,

at low tide
    ghost deer
    graze the rocks.
There is a star on the windowsill.

Everything glistens
    sand, stones, sea.
    Dreams surface
troublesome
    as seaweed
    tugging around ankles
coiling and curling in the heat–

so much heat
    the road is melting.
    At its end a track
then a cobbled path
    past deserted fields,
    old dreams,
mute stones beautiful in the sun

 – a relic chapel.
    Deep in buttercup grass

dreams unfurl
hang on yellow flags,

float on the flowers
    of mountain ash
drift in the scent of hidden bluebells.

Oyster-catcher cries
    skim the sea,
    on land the cuckoo
calls, calls, calls…..
    Those who left here
    could never imagine
the dreams of those who have come.

Susan Mobbs

Worth It Then

running for the boat from Seahouses
Farne Islands in our sights,
expanding your horizons
beyond the garden blackbirds that you loved.

That was the best day of my life
you told us as it ended,
up in the room in Berwick
where a swift flew through our open window.

Three thousand days were all you had
to match it with.
I wish you other days that will surpass it —

as hard to find, perhaps
as an islandful of puffins.

Elizabeth Bracken

The Gannet

Down plummeting down
Into a blue ocean
Gleaming white
No ripcord no reprieve
Free-falling

Diving all alone
White wings folded
Into a vast expanse of blue
A plunging speck
Of white energy

Julia Duke

Follow the gannet
White dart through sea sun plunging
Looking for supper

Lynne Nesbit

Where Has The Water Gone?

The trumpet whispers
the sigh of the sea.

Waves try to breathe
in gentle rhythm to and fro,
suffocate in each surge
of floating debris.

A curl of water attempts
but fails to escape
the kaleidoscopic quilt
smothering the shore.

Seabirds lie dying,
their stomachs full
of bottle tops, junk
ingested from the sea.

A drum beat knells
a world without birds.

Inspired by Hansu-Tori's performance of
'In Search of Common Paradise'

Sue Wallace-Shaddad

The Plastic Men

In the gouged earth
in the scoured reef
on the slicked beach
in the tunnelled earth
in the ragged breath of townsfolk
we have left our mark
but they will pass.

Earth will reclaim, refill, cleanse
change utterly
but eons will pass
before the plastic men
will relinquish their hold.

The drift and pull of moon-tide
will roil and tangle their flimsy grip
but not escape
they smother
they twine and twist
their granules lodge in secret places
poisoned
by their presence.

On and on
the long-dead plastic men
will grin and cling.

Elizabeth Soule

Balearic Shearwater

your trouble is, that few know
even your Manx cousin. If they saw you,
it would be a dark shape low over the sea
to be called a gull, if anything at all.
Indifference is the mother of decay.
Who gives a shit if a wood is felled to make
the train ride quicker from London to Brum?
The spotted flycatcher can commute.

Nightingale Avenue leads to *Curlew Drive*.
A wryneck fading in a glass case.
Sixty-seven species highlighted in ink,
the colour of blood.

Richard Whiting

            A large flint
                        falls out of a cliff
            A fulmar
                        has found a home

                        Margaret Seymour

Kitti-

Often confused for
Seagulls who are really gulls
We lie in their wake

Dide Siemmond

Recital on the Blyth

Reeds harbour nest sites
bearded tit, bunting, warbler
early summer's song.

Otter's silent path
spraint-marked territory
crosses river bank.

Low light intense glow
as dawn's first summer chorus
seeps through marsh and reeds.

Ann Follows

Feller

Regarding each tree he feels bark its fibres
its peeling beetle-burrow furrow and ridge
every snag flake gnarl rasp larval-nibble
to smooth to wedge to rake to hollow –
eyeing the leaves – the greens emerald jade
olive lime hooker's bottle viridian celadon
sea pea laurel; lacy skeletons hang here
their lineaments of death; sighting height
beneath vaulting sky - measuring trunk
girth thickness width girdling a self around
it bending a sallow a willow head sweeping
earth weeping over water for its sister ash
handle to the axe.

Pam Job

Magnetite

Tiny crystals of magnetite
clustered in a pigeon's beak
allow it to read Earth's magnetic field
and enable it to home

Nano-crystals of magnetite
have also been found in the ethmoid bone
between the eyes, just behind the human nose
A hunter-gatherer remnant
Vestigial, like the wings of an ostrich
How did we lose
our ability
to read the Earth?
our connection
to home?

Philip Baker

A Tanka from the Edge

Lost songs of my youth
loud chatter of tree sparrows
snipe drumming in Spring
the croak of roding woodcock
silenced by our thoughtlessness

Ivor Murrell

Eagle in Essex

September marvel
a white-tailed eagle wings hope
round our Essex home

Peter Sandberg

Hear how nightingales
blameless in their own demise
still sweeten our nights.

Eleanor J Vale

Linnet

she is at home in edgelands
where hedges thin to scrub

she sees our full world from
her ink-dark eye

her nest no larger than a
seedhead's dry bowl

in the lift and fall of her flight
she is light and swift as folded paper

gilded bars fade to species memory
all those tiny clicking locks just

held in her spindle-thin frame
as she stretches her breast-bone to the sun

Rosemary Appleton

Lines to A Linnet

Wordsworth found your trilling
sweet on the ear and brimming
with wise lore from the woods;
but were his words not meant
for you, song bard of open land?
I listen to your fast-paced melody
as I stroll past the only field of flax;
and turning, see a crimson crown.

Your avian lexicon is closed to me;
but when you sing, I feel the joy

until the music fades.

Caroline Gill

Stone Curlew

a ship on stilts
wades across dry land
subsides
like a cushion
on a stony hearth

Margaret Seymour

nest-stealer,
        who has stolen
        your song?

Species: Cuckoo (Cuculus canorus)

Caroline Gill

Cuckoo

Remember me, listen for
my voice calling from your childhood
over the buttercup fields
where the grass brushes your ankles
where you blow through your thumbs to
copy my call

how can I be lost?
what if I vanish from the language of children?
I am liquid ventriloquist
disembodied echo
my call is cavernous

marking the ticking clock of the earth
listen for me
two notes in perfect melancholy
a minor third cries to you
I nowhere have a home

Christina Buckton

Larksong : Three Haiku

A door to the day
spinning a necklace of sound
singing to save us

Threads of spun glass
hang then fall along the song
strong enough to lift us

Where's the quicksilver?
Dissect the small brown body:
only small song ghosts.

Christina Buckton

Skylarks sing and soar
high above the stubble fields
almost out of view

Eleanor J Vale

SKYLARKS

CAUTION
LIVE WIRES
OVERHEAD

Derek Adams

Keep Singing Us Back *

Over winter stubble
its barbed crest thrusts
to open day's door
taut notes twine into a necklace of sound
threads of spun glass strong enough to lift us
sing to save yourself to save us
hang then fall along the song
in a whisper of tiny gears
delicate as watch parts

open up the soft brown body
search among spindle bones

find the quicksilver

> * *They keep singing me back out of the dark days
> into sunlight*
>
> Jim Crumley, nature writer: *Skylight*

Christina Buckton

36

The Skylark

after The Crow by John Clare

A trilling quaver, soprano at its best,
I hear him warbling on the wing. It's true
he never seems to pause for any rest
and sings alone without the praise he's due,
his slender body almost out of view.
I see the brilliant sunshine tip his wings
so high above my head, the sky so blue.
I gather daisies to make bracelet rings
and watch him hang suspended as he sings.
I fall under the spell of summer too
and love to feel the breeze which sighs and swings
through uncut grass, an echo of my heart.
He pipes his tune, unwavering and free
as if to say, *just listen, follow me.*

Sue Wallace-Shaddad

Only the Crows Survive

The rabbits all drown and snakes recoil
and shrivel
deer leap over the edge, bears and lions
rage and roar,
burn up, and silver quietness
lures kangaroos
and crocodiles
to their death.
But corvids caress the wind
settling through the ash
to perch above this broken world.
A new beginning?

Sue Foster

Red List

Perdix cinerea is partridge, mottled brown, freckled front, sides barred chestnut.
Of the *Colombidae* clan, turtle dove noted for constancy makes earthy love-calls.
Finch-like corn bunting coded *Emberiza calandra* chit-chits and chuckles.
Of the genus *Motacilla* slender-billed yellow wagtail, another fêted farmland bird
Listed.

Wood warbler, lemon-yellow at the throat, from *Sylviidae*, trills at growing tempo.
On stiff wings, lark-like tree pipit – *Motacillidae* – parachutes when it sings.
Willow tit of *Paradae* progeny, repeats triple *zees*, perchance *ipse, ipse*.
Woodpecker – lesser spotted – *Dryobates minor*, plumage black, red, white
and humble dunnock among the country's woodland birds
Listed.

Even *Turdes merula* once common blackbird last songster of the day
and *Turdus musicus* fine-tuned throstle, speckle breasted
Listed.

If these were gone from Britain's shores, so too their airs, ambient hues,
numinous names – and what's more, they'd fade from every poet's word-store.

Antony Johae

39

Every Step

Every step I take, I elbow air, I break ground
Every word I say, I breathe heat, I commit mind
I spend sound. I am of this earth, I am of this sky
as much as is a blade of grass, an otter or a hoverfly

That I exist here at all is a miracle of evolution
but so too is a hawk's ultra-violet eye-razor resolution
I'm clever, but an Arctic tern, knowing instinctively how to fly
while burning minimal energy, its compass-mind its only guide
over featureless ocean, for thousands of miles, is surely just as clever
Only differently. But I am uniquely privileged - I have agency. I can decide
to be unconfined by the bounds of instinct, species, tribe, and go beyond them
Care beyond them. Intervene. And that is why I must come between, why I cannot
stand aside and let others take us step by step down the greenhouse spiral staircase
to extinction

Dide Siemmond

Earth

She began in cosmic dust and ashes.
What a triumph to mould herself
through aeons of gas and fire
wind, cloud, tumult and volcanic anger

to a blueness of joy
where tiny tendrils of life
have the power to crack stone
in their reach for the sun

where some of her children
pack a whole life into seconds
then give themselves to the creation
of cliffs and mountains, earth and rock.

Some of her children live for generations
feeding the air itself
watching history made and unmade
watching time grow and turn and change.

She is angry now
angry with feral offspring
cramming their mouths with forbidden fruit
breaking things they do not understand

but does she also love
these squabbling brats who have learnt
to build towers of passion
in her celebration?

Perhaps when we have tired her out
she will end it all
in ashes, dust
and a little glitter.

Elizabeth Soule

41

Suffolk Poetry Society is one of the oldest poetry groups in England and runs workshops, readings, an annual Festival of Suffolk Poetry and publishes the magazine *Twelve Rivers* twice a year. It has run The Crabbe Poetry competition since 1954 and an anthology of winning competition poems is published annually. The Society became a registered Charity in 2015. Its charitable objectives are to promote the art of poetry and the Society has entered into many projects seeking to explore the interface between poetry and other arts, collaborating with other organisations dedicated to the arts. This collection of poems is the latest of these projects.

suffolkpoetrysociety.org

The Lettering Arts Trust is the UK's leading voice for promoting the art of lettering to public and professional audiences. It champions excellence in the artforms of calligraphy, letterpress, etching and letter cutting by fostering talent, extending knowledge and facilitating new works. It brings the finest artists and the public together through exhibitions and events, original commissions and informal workshops. Its charitable purpose is to sustain the precious heritage craft of letter design and carving via formal apprenticeship, bursary and journeymen schemes that secure these skills for future generations. Based at Snape Maltings in Suffolk, there is a permanent gallery showcasing the work of renowned lettering artists, as well as a shop filled with unusual lettered gifts.

letteringartstrust.org.uk